Pam Carlisle

VENICE

INSIDE AND OUT

D0572528

(cover) The Grand Canal towards the Church of the Salute
View of the Grand Canal towards Rialto

VENICE
INSIDE AND OUT

CONTENTS

Pages 2-3:
St. Mark's Basin: Sunset
with a gondola

High water in St. Mark's Square

St. Mark's Basin with the Royal
Gardens and the Mint

PREFACE

This book contains a series of illustrations of the city of Venice in the following order: St. Mark's Square with views of the monuments and spaces which define it; St. Mark's Basilica with photographs following an itinerary from the left side of the exterior to the interior; the Ducal Palace following the usual route up to the Bridge of Sighs; St. Mark's Basin and the Grand Canal with the lateral "rii" (small canals) and the parts of the city closest to the Grand Canal as far as Rialto, and up to the railway station and Piazzale Roma (P). All the stops of the public transport system are given, together with the various lines which stop at them (for example, St. Mark's boat stop, n°15: Line 1 (Vaporetto), Line 2 (Motoscafo) and Line 34 (Tourist Service) stop here. The Friars' Church, the Basilica of SS. Giovanni e Paolo, the Ghetto, "Minor" Venice with typical and unusual sights, the islands of the lagoon such as Murano, Burano, Torcello and the Lido are also included. Each illustration is explained, and a brief note accompanies the visitor in the interiors and exteriors **INSIDE** *and* **OUT** *of the city: hence the subtitle of the book.*

This book has certain precise aims. Firstly, to make it possible for the visitor unfamiliar with Venice to move around the "calli" and use the public transport system in the most convenient way to reach the various monuments, islands and other places he wishes to visit, right from his arrival in Piazzale Roma or at the station; then, to point out or recall to memory the churches, palaces, museums and particular points of interest most worthy of attention; to remind the visitor on holiday, by means of a simple indication, of the fame of a particular painting, the originality of a certain space, the characteristics of the city's architecture and the importance of the lagoon environment, by means of a simple, brief note in the text; and lastly, to provide a reminder and souvenir to be taken home. Its aim is not to illustrate all Venice, which would be beyond the scope of any book, but to express the city's own particular taste, atmosphere and originality through photographs and brief notes.

Piazzetta San Marco, seen from the Basin

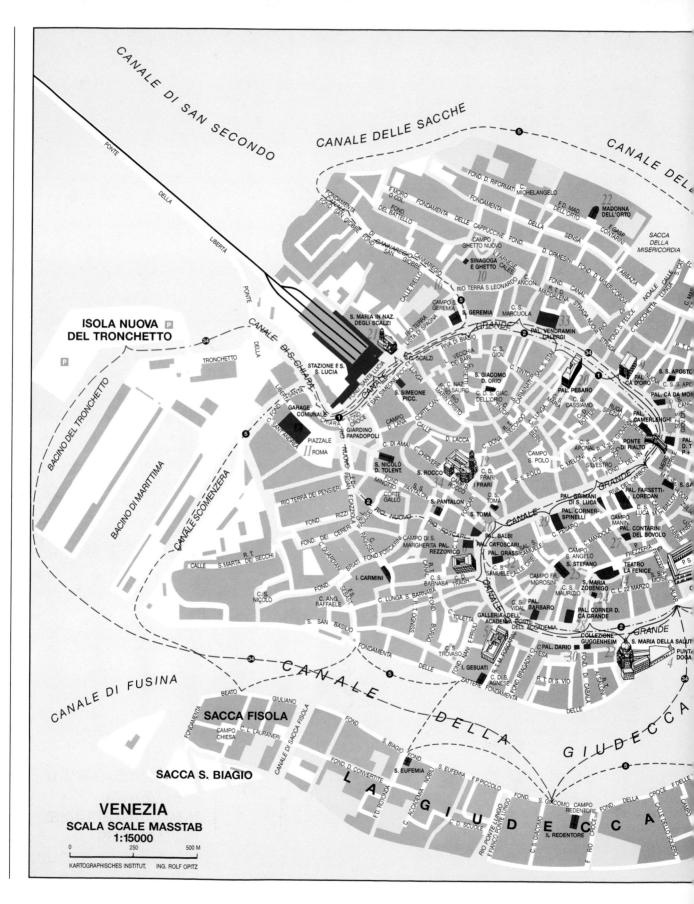

CANALE DI SAN SECONDO

CANALE DELLE SACCHE

CANALE DEL

ISOLA NUOVA DEL TRONCHETTO

BACINO DEL TRONCHETTO

BACINO DI MARITTIMA

CANALE DI FUSINA

CANALE

DELLA

LA GIUDECCA

GIUDECCA

SACCA FISOLA

SACCA S. BIAGIO

VENEZIA
SCALA SCALE MASSTAB
1:15000

0   250   500 M

KARTOGRAPHISCHES INSTITUT,   ING. ROLF OPITZ

MAP OF VENICE

1 ST. MARK'S SQUARE AND DUCAL PALACE
2 ST. MARK'S BASILICA
3 SAN GIORGIO
4 PUNTA DELLA DOGANA
5 ACADEMY
6 CÀ REZZONICO
7 RIALTO BRIDGE
8 CÀ DA MOSTO
9 CÀ D' ORO
10 THE GHETTO
11 PIAZZALE ROMA
12 CHURCH OF THE FRARI
13 CHURCH OF SS. GIOVANNI E PAOLO
14 LA FENICE THEATRE
15 CHURCH OF THE PIETÀ
16 CANNAREGIO
17 MURANO
18 CHURCH OF S. ZACCARIA
19 CHURCH OF SAN PIETRO
20 PALAZZO PESARO
21 CHURCH OF THE SCALZI
22 CHURCH OF MADONNA DELL'ORTO
23 CHURCH OF S. MARIA DELLA SALUTE
24 CHURCH OF S. MARIA ZOBENIGO
25 CHURCH OF S. STEFANO
26 PALAZZO BALBI
27 PALAZZO CONTARINI DEL BOVOLO
28 PALAZZO CORNER DELLA CÀ GRANDE
29 PALAZZO CORNER SPINELLI
30 PALAZZO DARIO
31 PALAZZO FARSETTI - LOREDAN
32 PALAZZO GRASSI
33 PALAZZO VENDRAMIN CALERGI
34 SAN ROCCO

MURANO

CANALE DEI MARANI

S. MICHELE

S. MICHELE

CANALE DELLE FONDAMENTA NUOVE

S. S. GIOVANNI E PAOLO

MON. COLL. BARTOLOMEO

CAMPO S.M. FORMOSA

S. MARIA FORMOSA

C.L.S. LORENZO

C.S. LORENZO

C. DELL'OLIO

C. DE CALION

C. DEI FURLANI

CAMPO D. CELESTIA

DARSENA ARSENALE GRANDE

C. MAGNO

S. GRECI

C. DELL'ARCO

SAL PIGNATER

MUSEO NAVALE

S. ZACCARIA

C. PIETÀ C. BAND. E MORO

CAMPO ARENALE

PONTE DEI SOSPIRI PAL. DUCALE

BIBLIOTECA MARCIANA

RIVA DEGLI SCHIAVONI

S. M. PIETÀ

ISOLA DI S. PIETRO

S. PIETRO APOSTOLO

CAMPO S. PIETRO

C. RUGA

PONTE DI QUINTAVALLE

FOND. DELLA TANA

CAMPO D. TANA

R. S. BIAGIO RIVA DEI SETTE MARTIRI VIA

VIALE GARIBALDI

C. CORRERA

SECCO MARINA

FOND. S. GIUSEPPE

VIALE TRENTO

V. TRIESTE

RIO T. S. GIUSEPPE

V. DE GIARDINI PUBBLICI

DARSENA DI S. ELENA

VIALE 24 MAGGIO V.

VIALE 4 NOVEMBRE

C. PASUBIO

C. M. SANTO

C. OSLAVIA

CAMPO STRINGARI

CAMPO SPORTIVO

V. S. ELENA

VIALE VITTORIO VENETO

PIAVE

4 NOVEMBRE

CANALE DI SAN MARCO

S. GIORGIO MAGGIORE

ISOLA SAN GIORGIO MAGGIORE

CANALE DI S. GIORGIO

TEATRO VERDE

PER LIDO

ST. MARK'S SQUARE

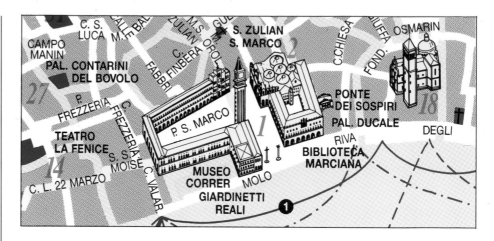

The **"Piazza"** is a famous space defined by famous buildings: at the far end the façade of St. Mark's Basilica, the Campanile standing alone and distinguished for its vertical thrust and the warm red of its brick, to the left and set back from the Piazza the Patriarchate with the upper section of the Clock Tower further to the fore and, even closer, the wing of the Procuratie Vecchie, with the Procuratie Nuove opposite, to the right. The paving of the square, in slabs of grey trachyte stone from the Euganean Hills, is enriched with a classical motif traced in slabs of marble. The Square itself is particularly spacious in a city like Venice where space is strictly limited in every direction, and in fact attained its present dimensions and form gradually over the centuries, for political and religious motives which outweighed the necessities of space for housing and other buildings. The Piazza and its continuation, the Piazzetta, constitute the religious and political centre of the city, as expressed in the Basilica, the Ducal Palace, the Procuratie - the offices and dwellings of magistrates - and the Library - a grandiose and prestigious monument to culture. The perfect equipoise of the various elements, and the exquisite refinement of the architectural details, express those qualities of serenity and magnificence which so characterised the Republic of the Serenissima.

Plan of St. Mark's Square

Piazzetta San Marco, from the corner of the Ducal Palace

St. Mark's Square

The **Campanile** is clearly detached from all the buildings around it. It has in fact had an architectural development quite separate from that of the other buildings, ever since the first watchtower was built for defence purposes in the area in the 9th century. As a defence tower it was conceived along military lines; an idea of how it looked may be gained from the mosaic of the "Construction of the Tower of Babel" in the narthex of the Basilica, on the left-hand arch of the main entrance. Finally, when the brick paving of the Piazza was replaced with grey trachyte at the beginning of the 18th century, it was left isolated, perhaps an essential element, with its particular colour and vertical thrust.

St. Mark's Square with the Basin and Punta della Dogana. Aerial view

The Loggetta by Jacopo Sansovino

Piazzetta San Marco, seen from the loggia of the Basilica

Pages 12-13:
St. Mark's Square, aerial view

The Clock Tower. The two Moors, two statues which strike the hour.

The upper part of their bodies rotates on a pivot and the hammers strike the bell. **"The Moors"** are famous both as a particular Venetian reference point and for the various literary allusions famous writers have made to the sound of the striking of the bell on the hour. **The Clock Tower.** The importance of this monument is best appreciated from the Quay and is heightened by its brilliant decorative effect and its function in closing off the line of buildings of the Procuratie. Interesting are the symbols of the city, of culture and religion.

The Clock Tower (detail)

Clock Tower, night view

The **cupola and the Campanile of San Marco.** These two essential elements of the Piazza, completely detached from any logical association with their environment, decorative and curvilinear the former, severely austere the latter, seem almost abstracted symbols of the Oriental and the Occidental worlds. For centuries divided, despite their common matrix, these worlds were brought together in Venice and reborn through the centuries of her history. Byzantium and Rome find in Venice another point of contact.

A cupola and the Campanile of San Marco

St. Mark's Basin night view

From the aerial photograph it is easy to appreciate the importance of St. Mark's Basin and St. Mark's Quay, also stressed by the buildings nearby. The gardens, now called the Royal Gardens, occupy the space once reserved for the state slaughterhouse and bakery. Beyond the small bridge to the lower left, in fact, stood the Fontego della Farina, the state flour stores. The area was however at the same time reserved for official ceremonies and as a fitting setting for these the Republic had a series of great buildings built by famous artists and architects: San Giorgio, the church of the Salute, the Punta della Dogana (customs house). Moreover it is here that one is most aware of how Venice looked towards and embraced the sea, her source of existence.

A view of the buildings overlooking the Basin

The Piazzetta seen from the Basin with the Clock Tower in the background

Riva degli Schiavoni

This celebrated painting shows St. Mark's Square as it was at the end of the 15th century and thus provides a comparison with later developments in the surrounding buildings. The most striking element is the façade of the Basilica itself, already complete in all the decorative elements which distinguish it. The columns of rare and precious marble, and the capitals, including the eight surmounting the columns of the main entrance, are gilded. The arches of the portal are decorated in gold and the antique cycle of mosaics in the lunettes depicts the arrival of the body of St. Mark in Venice. Today all the gilding has disappeared and the four right-hand mosaics have been replaced with works of the 17th and 18th centuries. Of the original mosaics only the one decorating the Sant'Alipio portal, the first from the left, remains. The mosaics in the large lunettes above have also been replaced during the course of the centuries. The four horses gleam in the centre of the façade. The Campanile is still set into the wing of the Byzantine building of the Orseolo Hospice; to the left the Procuratie are still the single-storeyed Byzantine edifices built by Doge Ziani. The Clock Tower has not yet been constructed. Typical Venetian chimneys top the buildings and the paving is still in brick: the entire scene is one of splendour and magnificence.

Galleries of the Accademia,
Gentile Bellini.
Procession of the Cross in
St. Mark's Square (1496).

Ducal Palace. Domenico Tintoretto, Doge Leonardo Loredan (1501-1521)

Pages 26-27. High water in Piazzetta San Marco

The Vogalonga

The **Vogalonga** ("long row"). The seemingly infinite number and variety of boats spread over the calm water of the Basin in front of the Punta della Dogana da Mar are taking part in the "Vogalonga". This typical word in the Venetian dialect, which means a "long row" over a number of kilometres, symbolises a return to the centuries-old Venetian tradition of water and oar. A few years ago, almost by unspoken common consent in recognition of a day of festivities and work together, all the boats in the city gathered at one point and the rowers, dressed in their everyday

clothes, began to row throughout the waters of the lagoon, almost as if the city had reawakened after centuries of forgetfulness to keep this traditional appointment. The following year the Vogalonga was organised in a more formal manner and students, craftsmen, clerks, builders, rich and poor prepared and trained in advance for the event, which had proved considerably demanding in terms of physical stamina the year before. The "Vogalonga" has now taken its rightful place as a major event in the life of the city.

ST. MARK'S BASILICA

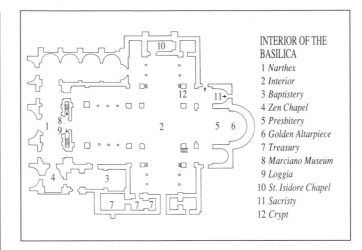

INTERIOR OF THE
BASILICA
1 *Narthex*
2 *Interior*
3 *Baptistery*
4 *Zen Chapel*
5 *Presbitery*
6 *Golden Altarpiece*
7 *Treasury*
8 *Marciano Museum*
9 *Loggia*
10 *St. Isidore Chapel*
11 *Sacristy*
12 *Crypt*

The **Basilica of San Marco** is the religious centre of the city of Venice. Before it stretches the vast space of the Piazza, and it is as if the interior of the church and the Square outside form a single cohesive unit, essentially one. The point of contact and integration of the two parts is the façade of the Basilica itself. With its decorative system more reminiscent of an interior it could almost function as the High Altar for the Piazza, which in turn becomes part of a church. The three exterior façades of the church, to the north (on the Piazzetta dei Leoncini), to the west and south, are so richly decorated with marble inlays that they must in past centuries have provided not only an embellishment to the façade, but a stimulus, a moral teaching and imposition of the glory and omnipotence of the Venetian state for the population able and in fact obliged to interpret the building in this light.

The various statues of saints, of diverse provenance and origin, the classical and mythological subject-matter of the reliefs (Hercules, figure of an Emperor), stress the idea of State and present it as a sacred, untouchable principle through the nobility and sanctity of tradition. Venetian women before the Basilica could be sure of the weight of divine authority in the healing of their ailments; the spiritual and cultural aura was such that no man could doubt for one moment his duty as loyal and complete subject of the Venetian state.

And then in the very centre of the façade, with their relentless forward thrust, were the four great gilded horses to call to mind, if necessary, the enormous power of the state.

Map of St. Mark's Basilica

St. Mark's Basilica

It was the Doge that elected the Patriarch and the bishops, and countenanced no interference on the part of the Roman church in the political affairs of the Republic. The population was well aware of this, and proud of it. The exterior of the Basilica, then, was the altar for the population in the Piazza and the interior and exterior spaces fuse into a single representation of the Venetian state. "St. Mark and the Lion!" was at once a religious exultation and a warcry, echoing for centuries in the Piazza and throughout the East. Gold, therefore, everywhere, including the exteriors, lavishly calculated to assure the entire population, the entire state, that Venice feared nothing. The interior confirms the concept of magnificence and uniqueness. The humble walls of brick are lined with gold and precious marbles; the state is present in the golden shields of all the doges since its foundation, expressing the continuity and immortality of the state, and the space encompassed is strange, at times undecipherable, suffused with the atmosphere of far-off, foreign worlds. The God who dominates the interior is the God of Law (apse, lunette and Golden Altarpiece) and the cycle of mosaics echoes a courtly art, of a world detached from the everyday, with figures whose physical form only provides a tenuous link with reality, but whose overall effect is one of incorporeal, dematerialised inhabitants of some metaphysical other world. And when, with the Renaissance, the mosaics assumed a more full-bodied, earthly character, politically Venice was to have completed her historic cycle.

In the year 832 the first church was dedicated to St. Mark the Evangelist whose remains, legend has it, were stolen from a monastery in Alexandria in Egypt by two Venetian sailors, and brought to Venice. The Evangelist's symbol, the winged lion, was adopted as the symbol of the city, with St. Mark as its patron saint. The church, called the Church of the Partecipazio because built by Angelo Partecipazio, whose family gave the city seven doges between 811 and 939, was destroyed in 976 when the populace set fire to the Ducal Palace during an uprising, to take doge Pietro IV Candiano. The next doge, Pietro Orseolo, began the restoration and rebuilding of the ruined buildings. In 1063, while Pietro Contarini was doge, work began for the rebuilding of the Basilica, and at his death in 1071 the basic fabric of the basilica was completed, its consecration occurring in 1094. This is the church we see today, but with constant successive embellishments, decoration, marble and mosaic facings. The finishing of the basilica was completed in the 15th century with the superb luxuriant foliage motif of the crowning.

St. Mark's Basilica.
Central portal, upper part

St. Mark's Basilica, main façade,
the Sant'Alipio portal

*St. Mark's Basilica,
the west or main façade.
Upper portion*

*St. Mark's Basilica.
The Cupolas*

*St. Mark's Basilica.
Pinnacles and the Campanile*

The **four large lunettes** of the upper part of the main façade of the Basilica are decorated with 17th century mosaics executed by A. Gaetano to cartoons by Maffio Verona of scenes from the Life of Christ. The most moving effect of these mosaics is the reflection of the light of the setting sun (the façade faces west) when they seem to come alive in a glory of dazzling colour and light. This effect may be seen, even from the Piazza, during late spring and summer afternoons. Towards the end of the 14th century the construction of the magnificent Gothic crowning motif of foliage and aedicules above the large lunettes was begun. Work was started under the direction of the Delle Masegne and continued later by numerous master sculptors, many of them Tuscan. In fact Tuscan artists were probably responsible for the majority of the decorations of the niches and statuary. Particularly important are the names of Nicolò Lamberti and his son Pietro, together with artists from his workshop. This was towards the beginning of the 15th century, when Humanist art was rapidly gaining ascendancy in Florence.

These horses, transported from the hippodrome of Constantinople by the Venetians in 1204 after the Venetian conquest during the Fourth Crusade, remain an enigma as to the date of their casting, the composition of the metal alloy, and their place of origin. Various hypotheses have been put forward, Greece and Rome, bronze and copper, 4th century B.C. and 2nd century A.D. etc., but still nothing can be said with certainty despite all efforts. What is certain, however, is their importance to the Venetian state over the centuries as a symbol of force and power. It was to neutralise this power among other reasons, that Napoleon had them carried off to Paris after his conquest of Venice. On their return to the city during the Austrian regime the horses were reinstated on the Basilica and continue to represent the tradition of the city.

St. Mark's Basilica, main façade.
The four horses in their traditional position on the façade

The four horses now in the Marciano Museum

Page 37.
St. Mark's Square seen from the roof of the Basilica

Piazzetta San Marco seen from the roof of the Basilica

Under the Republic, when the state wished to render official honour to a particularly important visitor, the guest was invited onto the balcony of the façade the better to admire the beauty of the Piazza and the Piazzetta. The same effect, with a somewhat exaggerated perspective, may be had from the roof of the Basilica. On certain summer days when great crowds of people fill the squares, the multicoloured figures become flickering spots of colour as in certain paintings by Guardi.

St. Mark's Basilica.
Narthex or atrium

St. Mark's Basilica.
Map of the Mosaics

St. Mark's Basilica, Narthex.
The Tower of Babel (mosaic)

St. Mark's Basilica, Narthex.
Cupola of the Creation.
Adam and Eve (mosaic)

The **narthex** provides an interval, almost a meditative pause between the open space of the Piazza and the enclosed interior. It is on a level with the paving of the Piazza and in fact seems to be a continuation of it under the Sant'Alipio portal, where only a simple marble slab marks the boundary. The narthex, both lateral sections of which originally reached as far as the transept, was modified in the 14th and 15th centuries to allow space for the Baptistery and the Zen Chapel on the right-hand, south side. The narthex also provides an introduction into the interior proper, as suggested by the decorations in the 12th-Century marble mosaic flooring, the mosaics of the vaults and cupolas, dating to the 13th century, with their subject-matter of Old Testament themes - the Creation-, the Flood, Noah and the Tower of Babel, Abraham, Joseph and Moses -, the precious columns, some set into the walls and serving as part of the architectural structure, others purely decorative, the marble slabs and the niches relieving the sense of the enormous weight of the walls.

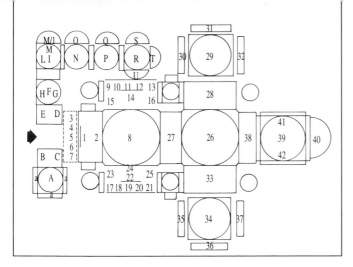

NARTHEX MOSAICS. A Dome: *The Creation of the World (13th century).* Lunettes A *Legends of Cain and Abel.* B, C Vault: *Legends of Noah and The Flood.* D, E Vault: *Legends of Noah and the Building of the Tower of Babel.* F, G, H Dome and Lunettes: *Legends of Abraham.* From I to Q Domes, Lunettes: *Legend of Joseph.* M/1 Lunette: *The Judgement of Solomon (executed by V. Bianchini, cartoons by J. Sansovino).* R, S, T, U, V. Domes, Lunettes: *Legends of Moses.*

INTERIOR MOSAICS. 1 *The Deesis.* 2 *Apocalypse Archway.* 3, 4, 5, 6, 7 *Scenes of the Last Judgement.* 8 *Pentecost.* 9, 10, 11, 12, 13, *Jesus flanked by the four Prophets.* 14 *Paradise.* 15, 16 *Stories of the Apostles.* 17, 18,19, 20, 21 *The Virgin flanked by the four Prophets.* 22 *Jesus praying in the Garden.* 23, 24, 25 *Stories of the Apostles.* 26 *Ascension.* 27 *Passion.* 28 *Miracles of Christ.* 29 *Cupola of St. John the Evangelist.* 30 *Stories of the Virgin and the Childhood of Jesus.* 31 *Miracles of Christ.* 32 *Episodes in the Life of Christ.* 33 *Scenes from the Life of Christ.* 34 *St. Leonard or Holy Sacrament Dome.* 35 *Episodes in the Life of the Virgin.* 36 *Four Saints.* 37 *Miracles of Christ.* 38 *Episodes in the Life of Christ.* 39 *Prophets proclaiming the religion of Christ (12th century).* 40 *Christ Blessing; below, the Patron Saints of Venice.* 41 *Episodes in the Life of St. Mark and St. Peter.* 42 *Episodes in the Life of St. Mark.*

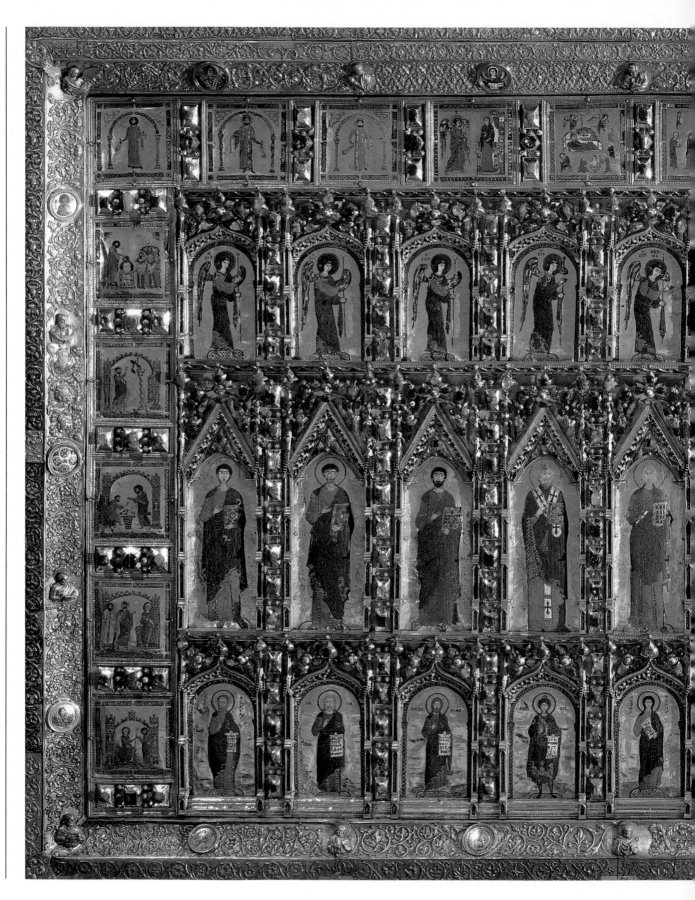

Entrance into Jerusalem

Resurrection

Pages 40-41-42. Golden Altarpiece. The central part

Crucifixion

Ascension

The **Golden Altarpiece** was the last work of art left intact at the fall of the Republic and today constitutes a testimony to the vast wealth of the state Treasury.

It is a singular, unique example of Gothic jeweller's art, measuring 3.50 x 1.40 metres, and inset with Oriental enamels of various eras, precious and semiprecious stones. The organisation of the screen, the

Pentecost   *Dormitio Virginis*

refinement of the details, the richness and age of the enamels and stones are a source of continuous wonder to the people visiting it.

The **Marciano Museum** (entrance from the landing of the central interior portal) houses an interesting collection of works of art and the Four Horses, and leads to the galleries and the exterior loggia of the façade.

·MARCVM·FVRANTVR·KANZIRhIIVOCIFERANTVR·

ALEXAN DRIA · THEODO R·PBR · STAVR CIVS MON · TRIBVN · RVSTIC · TRIBVN· · RVSTIC·

S · MAR CV ·

· CARNIB· ABSCONSV̄· VVERVNT·FVGIVNTQ·RETRORSV̄·

St. Mark's Basilica, apse.
Transport of St. Mark's body
(mosaic)

St. Mark's Basilica,
apse lunette.
Christ Pantocrator (mosaic)

IC XC

M·CCCCCVI
PETRVS
F.

Page 46. Golden Altarpiece. Angel

47

The **interior** of the basilica rests on a platform raised considerably above the level of the Piazza according to antique custom in the building of temples and basilicas, to stress the sanctity of the place. It has a Greek cross floorplan, of limited dimensions yet at the same time difficult to read or define. The flooring is in marble mosaic, the columns of rare marbles, the walls lined with slabs of marble in various colours below, and with mosaics in glass and gold above, as are the cupolas. One has the impression of walking over a rich Oriental carpet in various designs, surrounded by a half-light which accentuates the gleaming richness of the golden mosaics of the upper parts. The mosaics and their reflections seem to dissolve the contours of the arches and cupolas, multiplying the space. This is a profoundly religious building, once the chapel of the doges of Venice, and its origins are bound up in the history of this city poised between East and West, for centuries the all-powerful, greatly feared mistress of the Adriatic, of which it is the most potent symbol. It is Byzantine in its floorplan, its arches, cupolas, decoration and sense of opulence; Romanesque in its structure. Two worlds meet and combine to create a new, unique and inimitable masterpiece.

St. Mark's Basilica,
mosaic flooring (tinted design)

St. Mark's Basilica. Central nave

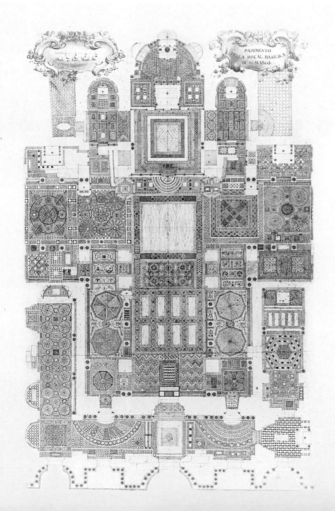

Space was taken for the **Baptistery** from the south end of the transept in the 14th century and even though it appears as a separate entity, it forms an essential and integral part of the church. It is between the Zen Chapel and the rooms housing the Treasury, on one side of the Piazzetta. The decoration of its interior was executed at intervals over a period of two centuries, the 15th and 16th. It was begun originally by Doge Andrea Dandolo, whose funeral monument, in the form of a hanging urn, is against the wall opposite the entrance (14th cent). During his term of office the Baptistery was organised as we still see it today and the mosaics which decorate the vaults and cupolas were executed. Previous to this the wall decorations, which seem to have dated to the 10th century, were frescoed. These mosaics, narrating episodes from the Life of Christ and the Life of John the Baptist, belong to the stream of popular Venetian art and are characterised by great expressive power as seen in the Baptism of Christ, and by certain Gothic traits - the ordering of the figures, the stylized representation of landscape, and the expressions of the faces. The Dance of Salome is the most typical and pure example of the style.

St. Mark's Basilica. Baptistery

St. Mark's Basilica. Baptistery The Dance of Salome (mosaic)

St. Mark's Basilica, south façade. The Tetrarchs

St. Mark's Basin night view

DUCAL PALACE

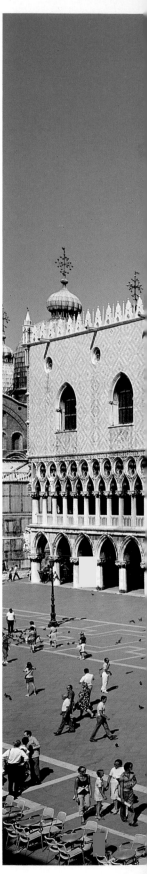

The **Ducal Palace** was begun in the second decade of the 9th century and the Republic of Venice spared no expense in embellishing both interior and exterior so as to present a fitting symbol of the ideal state. At first it resembled a castle and was primarily built for defensive purposes, assuming in Byzantine and particularly in Gothic times, more open architectural forms. The present building retains the Gothic forms of the 14th century, with wide, open loggias and windows which, together with the precious marble inlay covering of the walls, clearly demonstrate the security and wealth attained by the Venetian state. The Ducal Palace had certain well-defined functions. The section overlooking the canal comprised the Doge's apartment, with the following rooms dedicated to various Venetian magistracies such as the College and the Senate; further on were the Palace of Justice with various courts and the prisons, the "Pozzi" (wells) and the dreaded "Piombi" (literally, leads i.e. under the lead roof) and in the corner near the Ponte della Paglia, the Armoury. In the wing overlooking the Basin is the vast Great Council Hall, and in the wing overlooking the Piazzetta the Hall of Scrutiny. The Palace has a delicate, weightless quality, rather like lace, thanks to its softly coloured design motif, its pinnacles and aedicules.

The Ducal Palace, aerial view

The Ducal Palace.
Façade on the Piazzetta

From the photographs on these two pages one can clearly discern the very open character of the architectural forms and the enormously rich decoration of its façades. A continuous arcade with 38 sturdy columns surmounted by precious capitals opens onto the Piazzetta and the waterside. On the capitals, and in particular on those at the corners, are sculpted scenes stressing the role of the palace and of the state: symbols of commerce, of war and peace, while the marble group nearest the Porta della Carta depicts the "Judgement of Solomon", embodying the principle of Justice. The artistic level of several of the capitals has led to their being replaced "in situ" by copies, the originals being preserved inside the Museo dell'Opera.

The Ducal Palace, the Arcade.
The Loggia over looking the Basin

The Ducal Palace, corner facing the Piazzetta.
Adam and Eve (sculpture)

The Ducal Palace.
Roundel with the statue of Justice
overlooking the Piazzetta

Pages 58-59. The Ducal Palace.
Piazzetta façade, night view

Two arches on the upper floor correspond with each arch on the ground floor; each trilobate arch is surmounted by full and intersecting tracery circles forming a motif of crosses within the circles. The walls which spring from this base attain an effect of weightlessness thanks to the coloured marbles arranged to form a rhomboid motif, or open into large windows. From the large cornice above rise alternate white and pink pinnacles, each surmounted by drops of marble. The overall impression is of exotic, orientalising taste.

The Ducal Palace.
Porta della Carta

Main entrance or **Porta della Carta** (Paper gate). Above the architrave is the statue of doge Francesco Foscari kneeling before the winged lion; above the window is a bust of St. Mark, patron saint of the city, and at the top a statue of Justice with scales and sword. The sculptural decoration of the Porta della Carta was executed between 1438 and 1443 by Giovanni and Bartolomeo Bon, and painted and gilded.

The Ducal Palace,
Statues on the pinnacles
of the Foscari Arch

The Ducal Palace.
Giants' Staircase

The Ducal Palace. Courtyard

The Ducal Palace.
Golden Staircase

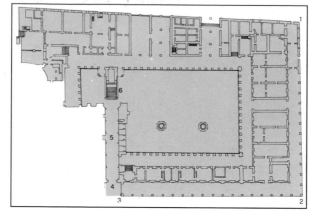

GROUND-FLOOR PLAN

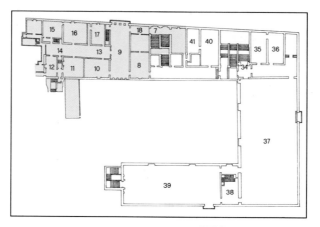

SECOND-FLOOR PLAN

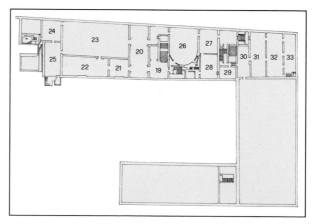

THIRD-FLOOR PLAN

A magnificent view of the Golden Staircase from the second landing looking down. The **Golden Staircase** was the official route along which one passed up to the various audience halls. It is decorated with stuccoes symbolising the power of Venice.

The Ducal Palace. Golden Staircase, ceiling stuccoes (detail)

The Ducal Palace. Grimani Hall

The Ducal Palace. G. B. Tiepolo, Venice and Neptune (detail)

Page 65. The Ducal Palace. Hall of the Four Doors

Hall of the Four Doors. The function of this hall, as a waiting and "clearing" room, is admirably expressed by the four doors placed symmetrically in the long walls. The hall is in the Palladian style and dates to the second half of the 16th century. The richly decorated stuccoed ceiling panels, by Giovanni Cambi and Maestro Baldissera, frame frescoes by Tintoretto depicting Venetian power.

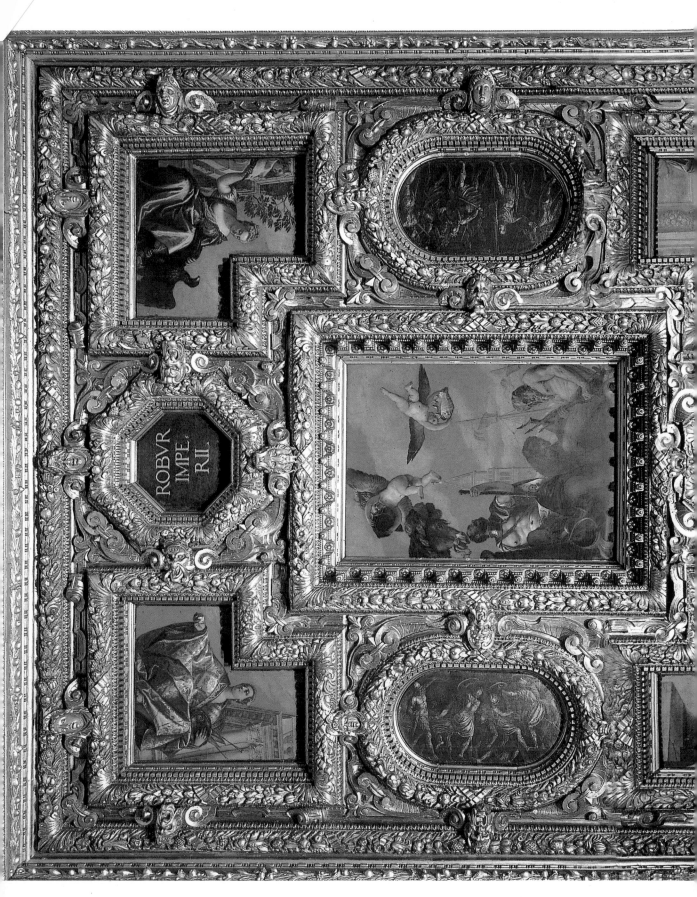

Hall of the Antecollege.
Jacopo Tintoretto, Vulcan's Forge

Hall of the Antecollege.
Jacopo Tintoretto, Mercury and the Graces

Hall of the Antecollege.
Jacopo Tintoretto, Pallas banishing Mars

Hall of the Antecollege.
Jacopo Tintoretto, The Discovery of Ariadne

Hall of the Antecollege. The chimney piece

The **Hall of the Antecollege** was used as an anteroom for the various embassies and delegations waiting for audience with the Signoria. The decorations on the walls, the chimney-piece, the frieze and the vaulted ceiling, with stuccoes, statues, columns, frescoes and mosaics with classical and mythological motifs, form a harmonious and united whole.

On the walls are several well known and prestigious canvases: Jacopo Tintoretto's "Vulcan's Forge", "Mercury and the Graces", "Pallas banishing Mars" and "The Discovery of Ariadne". These allegorical and mythological paintings, executed about 1577, are considered amongst the painter's finest works. Here too are Paolo Veronese's "Rape of Europa" and Jacopo Bassano's "Jacob's Return from Canaan".

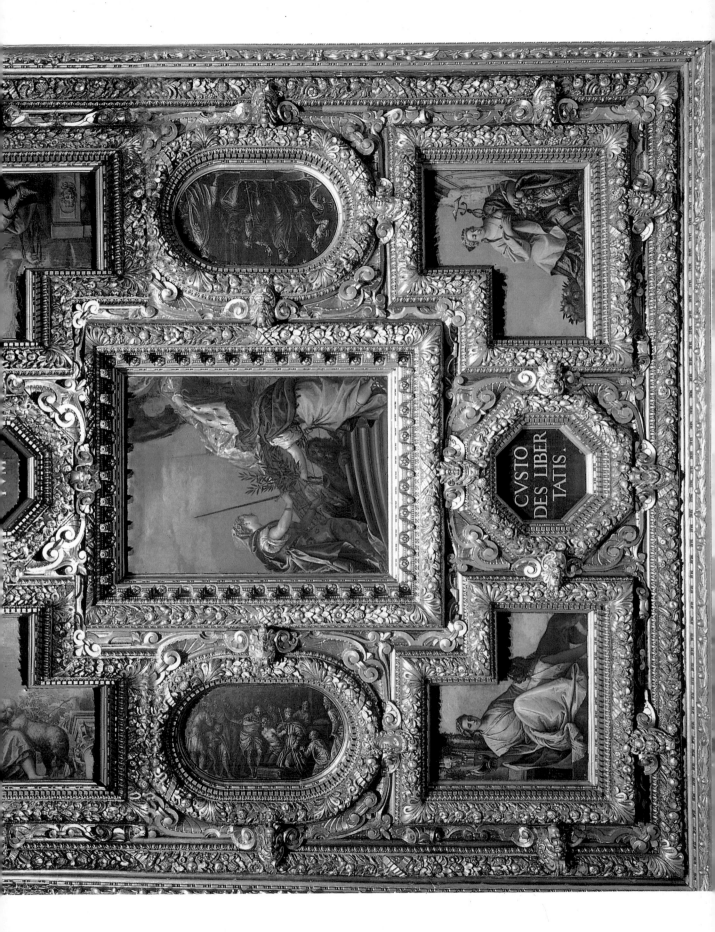

CVSTO
DES LIBER
TATIS.

Hall of the College. The magistrates who formed the College were responsible for the preparation and preliminary discussion of matters to be put to the Senate, dealings with the Roman Church and part of the judiciary power of the state, and for the reception of foreign embassies. The hall was decorated after the fire of 1574 by Palladio and G.A. Rusconi. The intaglio and gilded wooden ceiling executed by F. Bello and A. Faentin in 1577-78 contains paintings by Veronese, amongst which "Mars and Neptune", "Faith", "Justice and Peace render homage to Venice" and, amongst the symbolic figures, "Fidelity", "Prosperity", "Dialectic", "Meekness". On the walls are paintings by Jacopo Tintoretto, including "The Mystic Marriage of St. Catherine".

Senate Hall. The magistracy of the Senate was one of the most important in the Republic. Constituted in 1229, its members were limited in the 14th century to sixty, to which in later centuries were added the "Zonte", commissions comprising a variable number of patricians. This assembly deliberated all the political actions of the Republic, in particular decisions to declare war, the nomination of magistrates, the Patriarch and the Bishops, and study commissions to draft new laws and reforms in the various state departments. In Venice the members of the Senate were also known as the "Pregadi" because the Doge "prayed" them to enter the Senate Hall from the Hall of the Four Doors where they were waiting, at the beginning of each session. The room was decorated between 1580 and 1595. The ceiling, with its great panels and richly scrolled and gilded frames, was executed by Cristoforo Sorte around 1581. The paintings date to 1585-95, when Pasquale Cicogna was Doge, and include "Doge Venier and the subject cities" by J. Palma the Younger.

Pages 69-70-71, Hall of the College.
The ceiling (detail)

| *Senate Hall*

Hall of the Council of Ten. The magistracy of the Council of Ten was instituted in 1319 after the plot against the state instigated by Bajamonte Tiepolo. It consisted of ten members who enjoyed absolute jurisdiction over political crimes. The hall was decorated between 1553 and 1554 with canvases painted by G.B. Ponchino, G.B. Zelotti and P. Veronese.

The Ducal Palace, Hall of the Council of Ten.
P. Veronese, Venice receiving the Ducal Cap from Juno

Hall of the Bussola. This hall, literally the "hall of the Door Screen", was the antechamber of the Council of Ten and contained the "Lion's Mouth", a receptacle set into the wall into which secret denunciations could be dropped.

The Hall of the Three Leaders of the Council of Ten. Here was seated the Magistracy which originated in the Council itself. At first, before 1539, it was considered a supplement of the Council.

The Ducal Palace. Hall of the Bussola
The Ducal Palace. Hall of the Three Leaders

The Ducal Palace, Armoury. The Henry IV Room

The Ducal Palace, Armoury.
Gattamelata's equestrian armour

The Armoury. The Venetian Republic, always careful to maintain its political stability, had found it necessary to keep a deposit of arms inside the Palace itself. Thus any unexpected assault from outside could be faced at once. It is certain that as far back as the 13th century and perhaps even earlier, there existed an armoury in the Palace. The weapons, of various historical periods, were for everyday use in combat or were decorative and parade arms. There were also precious trophies and curiosities, the results of peace treaties, alliances and booty. The fall of the Republic marked the partial dispersion of this precious collection. Regardless of the fact that Venice was sacked, and in spite of the thefts after 1797, the collection is still rich and impressive. The Armoury today consists of 2031 pieces divided into various types: sidearms and firearms, arms for attack and defence, arms for combat, for jousts and parades.

Great Council Hall. This is the largest hall in the palace, measuring 54 x 25 x 12 metres. The Great Council was the greatest magistracy in the state and from the time of its inception on, increased in numbers from 300 to 1600. The decoration of the hall which we see today dates to 1578-95 and was effected by numerous artists, including Tintoretto, Veronese and Palma the Younger. The canvases depict the most important episodes in the history of Venice.

The Ducal Palace.
Great Council Hall

Hall of Scrutiny (Polling Hall). It was in this room that the votes of the Great Council were counted. It was constructed around the middle of the 15th century and badly damaged during the fire of 1577. Ten years later its restoration and redecoration had been completed. The intaglio work on the ceiling was executed to designs by Cristoforo Sorte and the paintings are by such Mannerist painters as Andrea Vicentino, Francesco Montemezzano, A. Vassilacchi l'Aliense and Camillo Ballini. They depict Venice's struggle against the other maritime republics. The paintings on the walls are "The Last Judgement" by J. Palma the Younger (entrance wall) and the Triumphal Arch by Andrea Tirali (end wall) erected in honour of Francesco Morosini, known as "the Peleponnesian" for his victories over the Turks during the Republic's period of decline. Outstanding amongst the paintings on the long walls are Tintoretto's "Conquest of Zara" (right wall) and "the Battle of Lepanto" by A. Vicentino.

The Ducal Palace. Hall of Scrutiny

The Ducal Palace, Hall of Scrutiny. Pietro Liberi, The Battle of the Dardanelles (detail)

The prisons, entry and exit stairways of the Bridge of Sighs

Bridge of Sighs

Bridge of Sighs. This bridge, constructed by Antonio Contin in the 17th century, enjoys widespread fame, thanks also to the attention paid it by writers of the Romantic and successive eras.

Love and physical suffering were intimately linked in their books and such tragic endings made a profound impression on the imagination of generations of readers.

THE BASIN AND THE GRAND CANAL

St. **Mark's Basin** is that expanse of water in front of the Molo (quay) of San Marco, with San Giorgio facing the island of Giudecca to the right; nearer to the right is the Punta della Dogana with the adjacent church of the Salute. San Giorgio, the Dogana (customs house) and the Salute may be considered three pearls ornamenting the entrance into Venice, the Quay. Our excursion along the Grand Canal begins here, and the gondolier will carry us gently up as far as the station and Piazzale Roma. Should we be fortunate enough to set out at sunset during the summer months, with that particular light and the water, the city would offer an unforgettable experience.

The island of San Giorgio seen from the Ducal Palace

St. Mark's Basin. View of San Giorgio from the Quay

Page 82. St. Mark's Basin with the Salute church and San Marco. Aerial view

Page 83. The island of San Giorgio. Aerial view

The island of San Giorgio seen from the Quay

The **Grand Canal** begins on the left-hand side, right at the Punta della Dogana, the point where merchandise arriving by water (Dogana da mar) were put through customs. On the right the canal begins at the San Marco boat stop (n. 15) where Line 1 (Vaporetto), Line 2 (Motoscafo) and Line 34 (Tourist Service) boats stop. The other boat stops up to the Accademia are Salute, n. 14 (Line 1), and Santa Maria del Giglio, n. 13 (Line 1). This first part of the Grand Canal, opening out into the Basin, shares with the latter its busy traffic of all kinds of boats, and its picturesque aspect. It was one of the first areas of the city to be settled, and the government of the Republic always paid particular attention to the Punta della Dogana. On the right bank are famous palaces such as Ca' Giustinian, Palazzo Treves de' Bonfili (17th century, B. Monopola); "inland" are the church of San Moisè, and the Palazzetto Contarini-Fasan, a Gothic building but anticipating the style of the Renaissance. On the left, the Punta della Dogana, like the prow of a ship, divides the waters of the Giudecca Canal from those of the Grand Canal. The quay opposite the Giudecca, at the back of the Punta della Dogana, is called the Zattere.

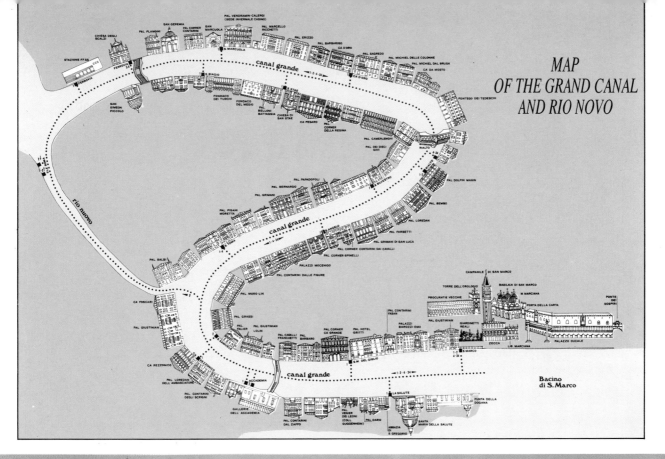

MAP
OF THE GRAND CANAL
AND RIO NOVO

STAZIONE FF.SS.

FERROVIA

CHIESA DEGLI SCALZI

PAL. FLANGINI

SAN GEREMIA

PAL. CORRER CONTARINI

SAN MARCUOLA

PAL. VENDRAMIN-CALERGI (SEDE INVERNALE CASINO)

PAL. MARCELLO RICCHETTI

PAL. ERIZZO

PAL. BARBARIGO

CA' D'ORO

PAL. SAGREDO

PAL. MICHIEL DELLE COLONNE

PAL. MICHIEL DAL BRUSA

CA' DA MOSTO

S. MARCUOLA

canal grande

SAN SIMEON PICCOLO

S. BIAGIO

FONDACO DEI TURCHI

PAL. BELLONI BATTAGGIA

FONDACO DEL MEGIO

CHIESA DI SAN STAE

CA' PESARO

PAL. CORNER DELLA REGINA

RIALTO

FONTEGO DEI TEDESCHI

rio nuovo

PAL. CAMERLENGHI

PAL. DEI DIECI SAVI

PAL. PAPADOPOLI

PAL. BERNARDO

PAL. GRIMANI

PAL. PISANI MORETTA

MOCENIGO

PAL. DOLFIN MANIN

PAL. BEMBO

PAL. LOREDAN

PAL. FARSETTI

PAL. GRIMANI DI SAN LUCA

PAL. CORNER CONTARINI DAI CAVALLI

PAL. CORNER-SPINELLI

PALAZZI MOCENIGO

PAL. CONTARINI DALLE FIGURE

PAL. BALBI

PAL. MORO-LIN

CA' FOSCARI

PAL. GRASSI

PAL. GIUSTINIAN

PAL. FALIER LOLIN

PAL. CAVALLI FRANCHETTI

PAL. BARBARO

PAL. CORNER CA' GRANDE

PAL. HOTEL GRITTI

PAL. GIUSTINIAN

PAL. CONTARINI FASAN

PALAZZI BAROZZI EMO

GIARDINETTI REALI

CAMPANILE DI SAN MARCO

TORRE DELL'OROLOGIO

PROCURATIE VECCHIE

BASILICA DI SAN MARCO

M. MARCIANA

PORTA DELLA CARTA

PONTE DEI SOSPIRI

ZECCA

LIB. MARCIANA

PALAZZO DUCALE

S. MARCO

CA' REZZONICO

PAL. LOREDAN DELL'AMBASCIATORE

PAL. CONTARINI DEGLI SCRIGNI

ACCADEMIA

canal grande

GALLERIE DELL'ACCADEMIA

PAL. CONTARINI DAL ZAFFO

PAL. VENIER DEI LEONI (COLL. GUGGENHEIM)

PAL. DARIO

S.M. DEL GIGLIO

LA SALUTE

ABBAZIA DI S. GREGORIO

SANTA MARIA DELLA SALUTE

PUNTA DELLA DOGANA

Bacino di S. Marco

The Punta della Dogana with the cupolas and bell-towers of the Salute. This point divides the Giudecca Canal from the Grand Canal to the right, flanked by splendid palaces

Grand Canal.
The Baroque Church of S. Maria della Salute

The area stretching from the Salute to the Academy on one side, and as far as the quays of the Zattere on the other, is one of the most picturcsque in the city, well worth a visit. There are small squares with fine well-heads, overlooked, for example by the façade of a Gothic church (Campo San Gregorio); narrow "calli" (Venetian for street) leading into wider "salizzade" (the first areas to have been paved -Venetian salizzar, Italian selciare, to pave); picturesque canals, and people talking, walking, stopping to look while a delicious smell of fried fish wafts out from the houses which are generally low, often single-storeyed, or one catches the pungent aroma of fresh fish from the fishmonger's stall.

One of the most characteristic canals in the area, near the Salute, is the Canale delle Torreselle, whose name dates to the 9th and 10th centuries, when towers and chains fixed to the sides of the canal were used in the defence of the city against pirate raids. The Canale di San Vio shows the entrance to Campo San Vio and the water-gate of Palazzo Cini.

Contarini-Fasan Palace

Dario Palace

Torreselle Canal

The Torreselle Canal (photographed from the opposite end)
has the cupolas and bell-towers of the Salute in the background.
It is a quiet canal, free of traffic.

Venier dei Leoni Palace, Guggenheim Museum

*Venier dei Leoni Palace, Guggenheim Museum.
Max Ernst, The Dressing of the Bride*

Palazzo Venier dei Leoni. The Palace is one of those gigantic mansions Venetian patricians built for themselves in the last period of the Republic. Its plans were drawn up by Lorenzo Boschetti in 1749 but the building was never completed. Its precincts contain a spacious Garden. Palace and Garden today are the seat of the Guggenheim Collection, a large private collection of Modern Art put together by Peggy Guggenheim, whose ashes were placed in an urn in the garden.

Barbarigo Palace and its façade decorated with mosaics

Rio San Vio

REGATTA DAY ON THE GRAND CANAL

The Regata Storica (Historic Regatta) is a municipal festivity celebrated down through the centuries with great pomp and circumstance, eagerly watched by Venetians and foreign visitors alike. The Regatta is preceded by a procession of large boats known as "bissone", all elegantly furnished and rowed by numerous oarsmen dressed in brilliantly coloured costumes matching the boats. The prows and poops of the boats are adorned with representations of maritime subjects. The doge himself, seated on the high poop of a large boat, travelled along the canal to receive the greetings of the people crowded along its edges.

The most comprehensive views of the regatta, held on the first Sunday in September, are to be seen from the Academy Bridge and the Rialto Bridge. The procession of boats preceding the regatta is seen against the background of the Basin and the Church of the Salute, with the opulent, richly decorated array, including the large boat which gives some idea of the magnificent barge on which the doge was seated for the event.

San Vidal. Campanile and Church

On the opposite side rises the Gothic church of Santa Maria della Carità and the former monastery, with the remaining wing of the cloisters built by Palladio around 1552 still overlooking the courtyard. The buildings now house the Art Academy.

Adjacent to the complex stands the former Scuola della Carità, once the headquarters of one of the six Scuole Grandi (Major Confraternities) of the city. Its halls have now been adapted to house the **Galleries of the Academy,** the most prestigious Venetian picture gallery.

The entrance portal leads off a "campo" which extends from the façade of the church to a small canal opposite, and to the boat stop (n°12) where Line 1, Line 2 and Line 34 boats stop.

The numerous rooms of the Gallery are arranged in chronological order from the 14th to the 18th century. Amongst its most celebrated treasures are, in Room IV, "St. George" by Andrea Mantegna, and a "St. Jerome" by Piero della Francesca; in Room V, paintings by Giovanni Bellini and Giorgione's "The Tempest" and "Portrait of an Old Woman"; "The Tempest", in particular marks an important innovation in taste and compositional concept in Venetian painting. In Room X, the "Feast in the House of Levi" by Paolo Veronese and the "Miracle of St. Mark" by Jacopo Tintoretto; in Room XVII, the Venetian view-painters (Canaletto, Francesco Guardi); in Rooms XX and XXI, paintings by Gentile Bellini and Vittore Carpaccio.

Galleries of the Academy.
Vittore Carpaccio, St. Ursula's Dream

*Galleries of the Academy. Giorgione, The Tempest.
In a landscape traversed by a stream, and with
strange buildings fading away into the distance,
a soldier stands looking at a half-naked young
woman, while a storm rages over the scene.*

*Galleries of the Academy. Vittore Carpaccio,
The Healing of the Madman at Rialto Bridge*

*Galleries of the Academy. Gentile Bellini,
Miracle of the Cross at San Lorenzo*

*Galleries of the Academy. Paolo Veronese.
Feast in the House of Levi*

Rio San Trovaso. Aerial view

Rio San Trovaso.
The Squero of San Trovaso,
one of the very few of its kind still
surviving in Venice

Grand Canal.
Palazzo Grassi

The gondolier takes us further along our journey up the Grand Canal. Over the centuries magnificent palaces sprang up on both sides. The first to the left is Palazzo Contarini degli Scrigni e Corfù, the second, visible although somewhat set back from the canal, is Palazzo Loredan, known as the Palazzo dell Ambasciatore, a 15th century Gothic building. To the right, in the foreground, is Palazzetto Falier with its typical lateral loggias, connected in Venetian architectural tradition with the "liagò" or solarium. Again on the left-hand side stands the imposing mass of Cà Rezzonico by Baldassare Longhena and Giorgio Massari, and further on Palazzo Giustinian and Foscari; famous as examples of ogival Gothic architectural forms, for the people who have lived in them, and for their importance in Venetian tradition. Palazzo Balbi which follows occupies a key position "at the bend" of the canal and at the entrance to the canal known as Rio Foscari which becomes Rio Novo leading to Piazzale Roma.

The gondola with two gondoliers provides a public service carrying people from one side of the Grand Canal to the other, known as the "traghetto" (ferry). In the past these "traghetti" were active at strategic points all along the Grand Canal and constituted a real moment of social encounter for citizens and the call of the gondoliers was a familiar sound for the people who lived nearby.

The **Museum of 18th century Venice,** housed in the rooms of Cà Rezzonico, comprises collections of furniture, sculpture and painting of the 18th century. The magnificent rooms, the superb furniture and the paintings recreate the characteristic atmosphere of the times and provide an insight into the patrician society destined for profound changes at very least, with the invasion of the Napoleonic armies and the ideals of the French Revolution. It is interesting to note the evolution of the portico on the ground floor, making an architectural comparison with Byzantine constructions, the arrangement of the great stairway leading up to the first floor and the immense ballroom leading off it and at right angles to the series of stairs overlooking the Grand Canal. Of particular note are the frescoes by G. Domenico Tiepolo and the marionette theatre.

Grand Canal. Cà Rezzonico
Cà Rezzonico. The Alcove Bedroom
Cà Rezzonico. The Ballroom

Rio San Barnaba
seen from Cà Rezzonico

The Grand Canal
towards Rialto. Aerial view

The Grand Canal.
Palazzi Balbi, Foscari,
Giustinian and Cà Rezzonico

The stretch of the Grand Canal from Cà Foscari to Rialto is of particular interest because it marks the boundary between the Sestiere (city quarter) of San Polo on the left-hand side, reaching as far as Piazzale Roma and the railway station, and the Sestiere of San Marco on the right. Along this section of the canal there were once three "traghetti", now reduced to two, at San Tomà and Riva del Carbon. In the "interior" an important foot traffic artery leads off from the market at Rialto. Here too are three public transport service boat stops: San Tomà, n°10, where Lines 1 and 34 stop, Sant'Angelo, n°9, where Line 1 boats stop, and San Silvestro, n °8, also on the Line 1 route. The area is also important for the nearby Rialto market. Particularly near the bridge there are buildings of the Byzantine era, and of successive Gothic, Early and High Renaissance eras. Various famous personages have lived in these palaces for various reasons: in Palazzo Centani, on Rio San Tomà, Carlo Goldoni was born and lived; in the 15th century Francesco Sforza, Duke of Milan, lived in Palazzo Bernardo on the left bank; in Palazzo Benzon, on the right bank after Rio Michiel, Countess Marina Querini-Benzon held her famous literary salons frequented by such poets as Foscolo, Pindemonte and Byron. The countess may be recognised as the model for the "biondina", a blond woman celebrated in several famous Venetian songs.

The **Rialto Bridge and the Rialto.** Construction of the bridge was completed in 1588: it links the two banks of the canal at its narrowest point and replaced an earlier drawbridge and a ferry, denoting the strategic importance of the site. Rialto is in fact the name of an area of Venice, the first part of the city to be settled and later the commercial centre of the most important city of the Mediterranean.

Rialto is the general name for both sides of the canal at this point; to the right is the part nearest San Marco, to the left is part of the market. The Rialto boat stop is naturally on the San Marco side. It is stop n °7, with the vaporetti of Line 1, the motoscafi of line 2 (terminus) and the Tourist Service Line 34 stopping here. It is the most convenient stop for those travelling to and fro between Piazzale Roma or the station and San Marco; a five-minute walk along one of the city's most important streets with its most luxurious shops, brings the visitor to San Marco. The left bank, usually known as Rialto, has more the atmosphere of the market, of fish, fruit and vegetables and general foodstuffs and some clothing shops. It was once a very important and powerful commercial centre. The photographs on these pages show various aspects of the Rialto, to demonstrate its enormous importance to the city in the past. For many centuries Venice had the name Rialto, deriving from the Latin Rivus Altus, deep water, and testifying to the most essential element for navigation within the lagoon, sufficient depth of water. Furthermore, Rialto today, the bridge, expresses the beauty of the city of which it is one of the best-known symbols.

Pages 102-103. Grand Canal. Rialto Bridge

Grand Canal. Rialto Bridge, with mooring poles in the foreground. The colours decorating these poles are those of the patrician family coats-of-arms from the palaces before which they stand

Grand Canal. Rialto. Fishmarket

Grand Canal. Rialto. The market area

Cà Da Mosto, in the photo above, is one of the oldest and best-preserved buildings in the city. The ground and first floors are typical of 13th century Veneto-Byzantine architecture, with high narrow arches, characteristic capitals and the open nature of the upper floor. The dwelling-cum-warehouse has remained intact, on the exterior at least, even in its decorative roundels and panels. The upper section was added in the 17th century. The name derives from the fact that the great seaman Alvise Da Mosto was born in the palace in 1432, and the early architectural forms indicate that the area was inhabited from ancient times.

Grand Canal. Palazzo da Mosto

Grand Canal. Palazzo Pesaro

Grand Canal. Palazzo Pesaro. Entrance

Palazzo Pesaro, Museum of Modern Art.
Vittorio Zecchin, A Thousand and One Nights

Cà d'Oro is the jewel of Venetian Gothic architecture and perhaps best embodies the essence of the Venetian spirit of those times - the 14th century - an exquisite decorative sense to the point of covering portions with gold, intricately interwoven arches repeating geometric motifs of circles and rectangles, beautiful marble facing, the cross motif decoration of the cornice, surmounted by marble spheres affixed with bolts at the top. The whole reflecting a particular moment in Venetian society when the fruit of long centuries of struggle could be enjoyed as wealth and security. The façade is still open onto the canal, to the water and the light, but not for strictly commercial purposes. It is just this tendency to divide the façade into two distinct parts, the upper more open than the lower, and even if dictated by lack of space (records show that it was impossible to extend the building to the left), it demonstrates the continuing tradition of the dwelling-cum-warehouse of the Byzantine era, although somewhat limited and reduced, on the exterior at least, to purely chromatic and decorative effects.

The interior, both in the entrance on the ground floor and in the first-floor hall, is reduced in size and embellished with marbles and paintings. It displays a clear intention on the part of the owner, Marin Contarini, to create a house in which to enjoy the wealth and comfort he had attained. The simple interior staircase with its exquisitely decorated balustrade, the precious window illuminating the hall, the loggias between the great mullions of the façade and the hall, confirm these impressions.

Thus, if the arrangement of the rooms, and what to us today seems insufficient lighting, remind us of a withdrawn, essentially Medieval atmosphere, yet the loggias seem to direct attention outwards, towards the life of the city, as was the custom in Venice.

Grand Canal. View of Cà d'Oro
Grand Canal. Cà d'Oro. The façade
Cà d'Oro, Franchetti Gallery. Tullio Lombardo, sculpture
Cà d'Oro, Franchetti Gallery. Titian, Venus

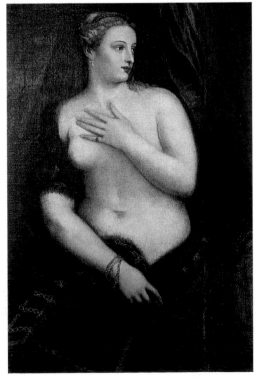

We are now passing through an area which could be defined as composite, of multifold aspects. The left bank, where the palaces in the photograph stand, has the Rialto as its natural focus. The names of the "calli" or lanes are "degli orefici" (goldsmiths), "della naranzeria" (orange sellers), "dei botteri" (cask makers), "del cappeller " (hatter), "dei raspi" (bunches of grapes) and indicate artisans, commerce and business, work. The private, civil and religious buildings are very ancient and still lend an atmosphere of evocative fascination: S. Giacomo di Rialto, Campo Santa Maria Mater Domini, San Stae, San Zan Degola (literally, St. John the Beheaded). The interiors of the churches and the architecture of famous palaces are renowned: in San Cassiano are several paintings by Tintoretto; in a building formerly occupying the site of the palazzo "della Regina" (of the queen), Caterina Cornaro, Queen of Cyprus was born; the original church of San Zan Degola dates to the year 1000. There is a typical building construction for civil purposes, the Fondaco del Megio (15th century) and nearby the Byzantine Fondaco dei Turchi, unfortunately much altered during "restoration" in the last century. A pedestrian route links this area of Rialto with the station and Piazzale Roma. The right bank has a very different, but just as characteristic, flavour. The area, through which runs the wide thoroughfare from SS. Apostoli to the station known as the Strada Nuova, was one of the latest developed. At its centre is the Ghetto, the Jewish quarter, with its high, narrow houses, once an important European Jewish cultural centre. The word "Ghetto" in fact derives from the Venetian "gettar", to fuse metal, the area formerly having been a centre of bronze foundries.

Grand Canal. Palazzo Corner della Regina, and Palazzo Pesaro

Grand Canal. Fondaco del Megio (15th c.)

Grand Canal. Fondaco dei Turchi (13th c.)

The boat stops along this stretch of the canal are: Cà d'Oro, n. 6, on Line 1; San Stae, n. 5, on Line 1, for the Modern Art Museum of Cà Pesaro and S. Maria Mater Domini; San Marcuola, n. 4, on Line 1 and 34, touristic Line, for the Ghetto; Riva di Biasio, n. 3, on Line 1; and the station (Ferrovia) n. 2 with three boat stops: one in front of the church of the Scalzi, on Line 2 and Line 34, another to the left of the church, on Line 5 "Circolare", and the other to the right as one comes out of the station, on Line 1 which travels the length of the Grand Canal.

Grand Canal, aerial view

Cannaregio Canal.
Palazzo Labia

Palazzo Labia. G. B. Tiepolo,
scene from the life of Anthony and Cleopatra (fresco)

Grand Canal. San Simeon Piccolo

Bridge and Church of the Scalzi

Railway station area, with the Bridge and Church of the Scalzi

We have thus ended our journey along the Grand Canal with our arrival at the modern access points to the city, the railway station and Piazzale Roma, the terminus for cars, buses and coaches. We are at the end of the Ponte della Libertà which carries both the railway and motorised traffic to the mainland. Modern life had to make some entry into Venice, and after the complete transformation of this ancient area of the city, extended still further, along Rio Novo in one direction and all around Piazzale Roma, destroying the past. A series of modern buildings, garages, parking spaces, docks and railway sidings, limited still in their function by the restricted space, have taken the place of churches, public buildings and private houses all testifying to the ancient civilization of Venice. There are various boat stops in the area: two are on Rio Novo. Boat stops on Line 1, 34 and 5 are around the corner at the beginning of the Grand Canal.

The **Church of the Frari** is an architectural element of the former monastic complex comprising two cloisters, the cells of the Franciscan monks and rooms for meetings and prayer. The complex as we see it today dates to the 14th, 15th and 16th centuries. The church is now visited by a large number of people, both for its architectural interest, in that its Gothic forms are punctuated by wide rhythms in both a horizontal and a vertical sense, and for its rich patrimony of works of art.

Foremost among them are Titian's Assumption of the Virgin and the Pesaro Madonna, Giovanni Bellini's exquisite triptych, Donatello's St. John the Baptist, a triptych by Bartolomeo Vivarini, the Monument to Doge Tron by Antonio Rizzo and a statue of John the Baptist by Sansovino.

Page 116. Friars' Church
Friars' Church. Monastic complex (aerial view)

Page 117. Friars' Church.
Titian, The Pesaro Altarpiece (detail)

Friars' Church. Titian, Assumption

Campo San Rocco. Church and Scuola Grande

Church of SS. Giovanni and Paolo

Campo SS. Giovanni and Paolo,
Andrea Verrocchio,
equestrian statue of Bartolomeo Colleoni

Page 119. Campiello Querini-Stampalia
Querini Stampalia Picture Gallery.
P. Longhi, Duck Hunt
La Fenice Theatre

SS. Giovanni e Paolo is the name of a noted monastic complex of the Dominican order, at the north-east of the city. The complex comprised the church, cloisters, gardens and meeting and prayer rooms. The Dominicans today perform services in the church, and the cloisters, gardens and conventual buildings have been given over to the city hospital, together with the buildings of the former Scuola di San Marco, adjacent to the church. Since the 13th century, when the order received land to build on in the area from Doge Jacopo Tiepolo, SS. Giovanni e Paolo increased continually in importance and prestige. The church early became a burial-place for many Doges and was enriched with prestigious works of art and funeral monuments, and as in many other parts of Italy and Europe became the "opposite number" of the Franciscan church of the Frari. The view from the square outside already provides a strong sense of beauty and majesty, with the simple pedestal of the extremely powerful figure of the mercenary general, Colleoni exemplifying courage and strength; the façade of the Scuola di San Marco with its sculptures and beautiful marbles, provides a note of refined elegance. The interior of the church repeats the movement of the Frari church, but is lighter thanks to the southern orientation of the apse. The most noteworthy works of art include a polyptych by G. Bellini, canvases by G.B. Piazzetta and P. Veronese, and the numerous funeral monuments ranged along the walls.

We have thus arrived at so-called "Minor Venice", lesser known but not for this less original and interesting, and perhaps more "immediate", tangible. This Venice offers unusual spatial solutions, such as these bridges at the Campiello Querini Stampalia. The palace has those marble strips connecting its balconies in widespread use throughout the city as decorative elements. The picture gallery contains a rich collection of paintings including a "Presentation in the Temple" by Giovanni Bellini and a "Judith" by V. Catena, as well as the exquisite "Duck Hunt in the Lagoon" by P. Longhi.

The **Theatre** enjoyed enormous popularity in Venice particularly during the 17th and 18th centuries, and there were numerous theatrical establishments sponsored by wealthy noblemen throughout the city. The Teatro La Fenice was built shortly before the fall of the Republic and its large auditorium reflected pure Baroque taste. This building was burnt down and in 1832 the Meduna brothers constructed the present building, retaining the Baroque decorative scheme of the auditorium but designing the other rooms in the Neoclassical style.

The **Church of the Pietà** or of the Visitation was designed in the 18th century by Giorgio Massari and was used as a concert auditorium as well as for religious functions. It has an oval floorplan and high in the walls are beautiful screens behind which the orphan girls, for a long period instructed in music and singing by Antonio Vivaldi, stood to sing. During this time the concerts held in the church of the Pietà were famous throughout Europe. The church has recently been magnificently restored to its original splendour.

The Zattere.
Church of the Gesuati

Riva degli Schiavoni.
Church of the Pietà

Palazzo Ariani at
Angelo Raffaele.

Campo Manin.
Palazzo Contarini
del Bovolo

Palazzo Ariani at Angelo Raffaele dates to the second half of the 14th century. Its great mullioned window was the first of the kind in Venice and served as a model for later buildings.
Palazzo Contarini del Bovolo, with its superb spiral staircase, is a Renaissance building constructed by G. Candi in 1499. The staircase, withdrawn, rises in the small campo and provides an unexpected sight as one turns the corner; this fact, besides the originality of its design, has contributed to its fame.

The densely inhabited "sestiere" of **Cannaregio,** built over long narrow islands intersected by parallel canals and with quays running along them, has its own particular charm, unlike that of any other area of the city. The buildings are Gothic, Renaissance and Baroque, with no traces of earlier styles, not even of the Byzantine period, the area not having been developed at the time. In 1516 a state decree ordered that all Jews be concentrated and indeed enclosed in the area known as the "getto". The derivation of the word **"ghetto"** may be traced to the foundries for fusing (Venetian "gettar") bombards which flourished in the area.

Cannaregio, campo di Ghetto Nuovo

Church of the Madonna dell'Orto

Church and Scuola della Misericordia

Rio Santa Caterina

MURANO

Amongst the islands of the lagoon, many of which have disappeared over the centuries while others have emerged and formed, Murano is one of the most famous. This fame is to a large degree due to the traditional production of glass there, which is known as Murano glass. The historical origins of this production on Murano are not known; in the beginning it appears that glass was produced in Venice itself, but a state decree ordered the removal of the furnaces to Murano because of the number of fires they had caused in the city. This occurred from the 12th to the 13th century, but Murano had already served as a place of refuge for fugitives from the mainland and in later centuries the Venetian nobility built villas, monasteries and churches on the island.

BURANO

The island of Burano has made no distinctive mark on the history of the people of the lagoon; it has neither ancient traditions nor noteworthy monuments. It is thus to be presumed that for centuries it remained a hamlet of fishermen and others connected with the sea, and in fact it is still basically a fishing village. But another activity has proved singularly important: lacemarking, with which the women would occupy themselves as they awaited the return of their menfolk.

Burano should be visited with this important fact in mind, to fully appreciate the small houses, the cadence of the dialect, the perfect union of water, man and environment.

Page 122. Murano Church of S. Maria e Donato (12th c.)

Graceful examples of Murano glass

Burano. Views

TORCELLO

Torcello is an island very close to Burano, but it remains, solitary and humble as it appears today, one of the most important centres of the origin of the Venetian state. Its importance for the fugitives from the mainland seeking some place offering sufficient security for settlement, was dictated by its position in respect to the mainland. The fugitives who settled here came from Altino, fleeing before the Longobard hordes, and brought with them the sacred remains of their patron saint from their abandoned city, naming it Torcello from the Tower (Italian "torre"), symbol of their lost homeland. They also brought with them their habits and customs, their language and their laws and the entire social structure which had regulated their lives together until that moment. And lastly they brought an artistic tradition, of classical origins. On Torcello they built a house of God and a Baptistery, and their own houses clustered around them, rude and poor certainly in the beginning, but increasingly grand as they began to trade and do business, to organise a new kind of life in the middle of the water. The visitor to Torcello is immediately struck by the whole environment - water, mudflats, flights of birds, solitude - and by the extreme nobility of the 11th-century campanile, despite its simplicity, and of the 11th-century cathedral of S. Maria Assunta and the 11th-12th-century church of S. Fosca. In front of the cathedral are the remains of the 7th-century Baptistery; inside, a superb mosaic covering the end wall and dignified architectural forms, and a powerful mosaic of the Virgin at once mystical, ethereal, metaphysical.

Torcello, the Square
Island of Torcello
Torcello, Cathedral. Last Judgement (mosaic)
Torcello, a canal

CHIOGGIA

An excursion to Chioggia, whether by bus or by waterbus, provides the opportunity to take in the littoral, the Murazzi, and, should one stop off at S. Pietro in Volta, the life of the fisherfolk. Chioggia today is a fishing port but tradition certainly dates back to Roman times. It was then called Fossa Clodia Maggiore and Chioggia Minore or Sottomarina. The Chioggian War (1378-80) was a turning point in the history of the Republic. Besieged by the Genoese fleet, and on the point of yielding, Venice made a last effort and was rewarded with victory. Among the ancient buildings in Chioggia, mention must be made of the church of S. Domenico, with Vittore Carpaccio's painting of St. Paul (1520), the church of S. Giacomo and the Cathedral with its-bell-tower. The Cathedral,with nave, two aisles and transept, was originally built to a basilican plan. Sottomarina is a modern seaside resort in constant evolution.

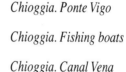

Chioggia. Ponte Vigo

Chioggia. Fishing boats

Chioggia. Canal Vena

Chioggia. Canale Lombardo

Venice, a typical view.
Cannaregio, the Bridge with
the three arches

The Lagoon of Venice.
Island of San Francesco del Deserto

OPENING HOURS

(W.= Weekdays   H.= Holidays)

Academy (Tel. 5222247) W. 9 - 14; H. 9 - 13 L. 8000
St. Mark's Basilica (Tel. 5225205). *Campanile*
May - Sept.: 9,30 - 20; Oct. - Apr.: 10 - 16 L. 4000
Gallery and Museum May - Sept.: 9,30 - 17; Oct. - Apr.: 10 - 16 L. 2000
Pala d'Oro and Treasury May - Sept.: 9,30 - 17
Oct. - Apr.: 10 - 16 L. 2000
Cà d'Oro (Tel. 5238790) W. 9 - 13,30; H. 9 - 12,30
(Ticket office closes 1/2 h. before closing time)
Closed 1/1 - 1/5 - 25/12 L. 4000
Cà Rezzonico (Tel. 5224543). Apr. - Oct.: 9 -19;
Nov. - March: 9 - 16 Closed Fridays; 1/1 - 1/5 - 25/12
L. 5000 (Discount for students)
Campanile of S. Giorgio (Tel. 5289900) Apr. - Oct.: 9,30 -18,30
Nov. - March: 9 - 12; 14,30 - 17,30 L. 2000
Modern Art Museum of Cà Pesaro (Tel. 721127)
10 - 16 Closed Mondays L.3000
Guggenheim Collection (Tel. 5206288) W.11-18;
Saturdays: 11 - 21 (18 - 21 Free entrance) Closed Tuesdays L. 7000
Ducal Palace (Tel. 5224951) Apr. - Sept.: 9 - 19
Oct. - March: 9 - 16 (Ticket office closes 1 h. before closing time)
Closed 1/1 - 1/5 - 25-26/12 L. 8000, (students L. 4000)
Scuola S. Rocco (Tel. 5234864) Apr. - Oct.: 9 - 13; 15,30 - 18
Nov. - March: W. 10 - 13 Closed 1/1 - Easter - 21/11 - 25/12 L. 7000

The publisher wishes to thank the Procuratoria San Marco for its kind permission to reproduce the photographs of the Golden Altarpiece on pages 40-41-42-43-44-45-46.

STORTI EDIZIONI

Via Miranese, 104 La Fossa di Mirano, Venezia - C.P. 361 30170 Mestre P.T. VE
Tel. 041/431607 Fax 041/432347

Photography: ARCHIVIO STORTI,
CAMERAPHOTO, GIACOMELLI

Printed: March 1994

Cover: Venice. San Giorgio